Fine as Frog's Hair

Steven Landau, M.D.

ISBN 978-0-557-18875-8

FOREWORD

When first I came to Johnston County in 1986, I was astounded at the colorful dialect that was used by my patients, young and old. Over the years, as cosmopolitan influences developed, that dialect became less common. So I decided to share my delight in these wonderful idioms with all of you who would like to enjoy them as much as I do.

The illustrations were done by V. Cullum Rogers, and are a tribute to his talent and imagination. Cullum is a freelance cartoonist and caricaturist in Durham, North Carolina. His work appears regularly in *The Independent Weekly* and can be seen at www.vcrogers.com.

Jeannie Woodard did the cover painting of the tobacco barn, and has many such works of art which are on sale at places around Johnston county. You may also contact her at (919)-284-5638 to get some of her great pieces. When my patients see her paintings hanging in my office, they commonly say things like "That's the old tobacco barn, straight up and down! Reminds me of when I was a boy on my Daddy's farm!"

This book would not have been printed without the input of the good people of Johnston County, North Carolina, who gave me the ideas and the vocabulary and patiently explained to me what they were talking about. Thanks go to my wife, Ellen, and my son, Joshua, for assistance with proofreading; to my office staff members Carol Webster, Johnna Moore and Edna Bernheisel, for their additions and critical comments; to Ric Moore (Rakesh) for pointing me to a proper publisher, and to Scotty Cherryholmes, for help with assembling the cover art.

Finally, all credit goes to my guru, P.R. Sarkar, founder of the Ananda Marga Yoga Society, for having first done his own version of this type of lexicon in the Bengali language. He requested us to study our own languages and those of others, and inspired me to perform this "labor of love" myself.

You may reach me at my office at (919)-209-9930, or by email at pashupati@bellsouth.net, and access my music CD entitled "Spiritual Smatterings," and my "Yoga for All" DVD. Please also visit my website at www.shivadancing.com to access other publications, including my father's Holocaust Memoirs.

Best wishes to all,

Steven Landau, M.D.

"I'd rather eat a peck of boogers."

WORD	MEANING	EXAMPLE
'longs	belongs	He jist don't have all that 'longs to him.
a day and a night	24 hours	I don't smoke much - not more'n a pack in a day and a night.
a heap	a whole lot	He's got a heap more money now than he did last year.
a long dry spell	a hard time	After my wife died was a long dry spell for me and the kids.
a peck of boogers	bad thing	I'd rather eat a peck of boogers than be working here now.
a sight	much	He's a sight smarter now since he come back home from college.
a week to die sudden	real slow	I'm getting so slow it'll take me a week to die sudden.
a-squealin'	wheezing	I was a-squealin' in my chest so bad I thought I'd die.
ain't right	not sane, not functioning well	She ain't been right since the car hit her.
all manner	all types	He brought in a pot with all manner of vegetables.
anything that don't bite me first	I have a good appetite	I can eat anything that don't bite me first.
Anna Bell's Café	ABC store	Where's Pop? At Anna Bell's Café.

arsh potatoes	Irish potatoes, new potatoes	We just brought in a crop of arsh potatoes; they're good!
Arthur	arthritis	Ol' Arthur's got me good, Doc. You got anything for that?
at the time	right now	I can't find none at the time.
automatic	it naturally follows	It's automatic that doctor messed up, cause two other folks got the same infection from him.
ABC store	Alcoholic Beverage Control store	I supply gin-soaked raisins from the ABC store.
All-American Boy's College	ABC store	Your boy went to Harvard? Well, my Junior's going to graduate from the All-American Boys' College.
backer	tobacco	He was chewin' backer and let fly a squirt to kill a toad.
bad for	famous for	He's bad for burping in public
ballin' the jack	speeding	He was ballin' the jack heading down to Florida.
banches	benches	Fetch me them banches from over yonder.
barefoot as a yard dog	unshod	You're barefoot as a yard dog! Get some slippers on afore you catch your death of cold!

barf ugly	very unsightly	You want me to date Ellie Mae? But she's barf ugly and smells bad!
barrel of sense	good brains	That doctor's got a barrel of sense.
barreling down	trying hard	He was barreling down at the prom, but someone else won the prize pig.
bate	large quantity	Last night I ate me a bate of pork chops; they was good.
begged like a dog	pleaded strongly	I begged him like a dog to quit smokin', and now he's dead.
behind	after	We lit them fireworks one behind the t'other.
between the ditches	drive straight	In Rescue, we used to just try to keep it between the ditches.
big	fat	She's a big girl but she's sure pretty.
big as Baylock's bull	very big	Mom was bigger'n Baylock's bull.
big ol'	very large	I got me a big ol' slab of ham 'n' some biscuits 'n' coffee.

bless his heart	poor fellow	Bless his heart, he can't do no better.
blessed out	cussed out	Daddy blessed me out good after I wrecked his car.
blessed Pat	damned	Well, I'll be blessed Pat!
boo-boos	sorry, low-class people	They're just a bunch of boo-boos.
boot	trunk of the car	I was selling my strawberries out of the boot.
borrowed mule	object worthy of exploitation	He run me like a borrowed mule.

bow-legged mule	slow	If he gets any slower, I'll buy him a bow-legged mule.
break it down	explain it	I like you Doc, 'cause you break it down to me.
broke down with me	got to me badly	That flu bug broke down with me.
broke as a convict	impecunious	That flood left me broke as a convict.
brung	brought	Daddy brung Mama home in the back of the pickup.
buck fever	catastrophic confusion brought on by confrontation with a 14 point buck deer	Johnnie got buck fever first time he met Sue.
budgies	restless legs syndrome	Doc, have you got somep'n for the budgies?
burn	glow	My left headlight don't burn so good no more.
cake of soap	very small	That baby weren't no bigger than a cake of soap with a week's worth of washing off it.
can't hardly	can hardly	I can't hardly sit up, I'm so weak.
case the joint	look things over	I cased the joint before I moved in.

cha-hoots	collaboration	They're in cha-hoots over selling that washed-up truck.
checks you up	stops your symptoms	That Pepto-Bismol sure checked up my runs.
chunk	throw	Chunk that ball over here.
chunk	toss, throw away	Chunk it boy, it's worthless.
clean	completely	That pinched nerve burned from my neck clean down my arm.
clumb	climbed	He clumb up that pole jes' as neat as a cat.
cold-natured	tending to be chilly	I'm cold-natured, and I keep the heat up high.
come on	come now	We have no appointments left open. Just come on and we'll work you in.
coming	growing, expanding	I've got a coming appetite.
cotton to	prefer	I don't cotton to his messin' with her in that barn.
couldn't live and couldn't die	felt real bad	I was so sick I couldn't live and I couldn't die.

crackles like a saddle	joint crepitus	My knees crackle like a saddle every time I bend down to pick something up.
cures all, kills none	good doctor	He's a good doctor; cures all, kills none.
curious	strange, inappropriate	It's curious that you should tell me to quit smoking in my own house.
cuss a cat out	do something small	There's not enough room here to cuss a cat out.
cut a rug	dance hard or well	Dr. Landau was cutting a rug at the Moose Lodge party. Did you see him?
cut the lights on	turn the lights on	Cut the lights on, honey.
cutting a buck	dancing fast	Sue was cutting a buck with Robby, and then she fainted.
Daddy rabbit	large, authoritative	That screwdriver's too small. I need the Daddy rabbit for this one.
dead ache	constant, dull ache	I just had a dead ache in my chest.
dead as a hammer	inactive	My cell phone just quit. It's dead as a hammer.
dead man needs a coffin	desperate need	I need a dentist worse than a dead man needs a coffin.

dead pig in the sunshine	contented	I'm just as happy as a dead pig in the sunshine.
Dick's hatband	very tight	My legs were swollen up tighter than Dick's hatband.
dinner	lunch	After dinner, I'm going back to work till sunset.
directly	in the near future; soon	I'll be there directly.
dizzy-headed	dizzy	My heart beat quick-like, and then I got right dizzy-headed.
dizzy-like	dizzy-headed, vertiginous	I got dizzy-like for awhile, then I settled down and rested.
doodle, happy as a	lighthearted and carefree	We been happy as a doodle since moving to our own apartment.
doololly	thingamajig	Fetch me that doololly from over yonder.
dootcher	do what your	Doothcher mother says, boy.
down the country	a hard time	The sheriff gave me down the country for beating my boy.
down to the short rows	nearly done	Only 20 charts left to review. Reckon we're down to the short rows.
draw up	contract	My toes draw up at night and I can't hardly sleep.
draw a breath	take a breath	It hurts whenever I draw a long breath.

drawing up	contracting	My toes draw up at night and I can hardly sleep a wink.
dressed down	dressed up	He was all dressed down, neater'n a pin.
drinks gas	guzzles gas	Does your car drink gas like mine does?
dry as gunpowder	very dry	My mouth was dry as gunpowder after taking those antidepressants.
dry as a powder house	very dry	see above
duck-legged	bow-legged	Her mamma was kindly duck-legged.
eat up	consumed	He's all eat up with cancer.
eatin' the hinges off'n the doors	very hungry, good appetite	Hungry? He's eatin' the hinges off'n the doors.
elevator doesn't go all the way up	stupid, a bit crazy	Her elevator doesn't go all the way up.
evening	afternoon	Are you open this evening, Doc?

ever what	whatever	Ever what you say, Doc, I'll do it.
ever who	whoever	Ever who talked to me was real mean.
every two days	every three days	Give him an enema if he doesn't have a BM every two days.
evidently	we have proof	Evidently he came back, 'cause his gloves are here.
eyeball	precious one	That's my grandyoung'un. She's my eyeball.
extra	great	"How ya feelin', Joe?" "Extra!"
falling apart	ageing severely	Doc, I've got Arthur bad, heart dropsy and a touch of the sugar. Reckon I'm just falling apart!
fall off	lose weight	Pa's been fallin' off lately Doc. Reckon vitamins'd help?
fall out	faint	She got too hot, and fell out in the field.

fannin' the covers	having sex	They was a-fannin' the covers all night long.
favors	looks like	Your son Joshua sure favors you.
fell dead	dropped dead	Mortimer fell dead last week.
fifth and the fourth	May fourth	I got hit by a car on the fifth and the fourth of last year.
fighting fires	really busy	It's fighting fires around here.
fine as frog hair	very well	I'm feeling fine as frog hair split three ways!
fixin' to	about to	I'm fixin' to call the ICU right now.
flame	phlegm	Just coughed up some yaller flame, Doc. Want it?

flew all over me	consumed me	That flu bug just flew all over me somethin' bad.
flew mad	exploded in rage	When he talked about Momma, I flew mad at him.
floor pen	low rank (from pig farming)	I see you're still on the floor pen.
flusterated	frustrated and flustered	I get flusterated every time I try to talk French.
fly flap	fly swatter	I got me a fly flap for those skeeters.
founder	collapse	I'll founder after this dinner.
frog	sole of the foot	He had an ache in the frog of his foot.
furniture moving	I'm moving slowly	The furniture in the house was moving faster than me!
gag a maggot	revolting	It was enough to gag a maggot.
get better to die	feel real bad	I'm so bad off I'd have to get better to die.
get-go	beginning	He knew she was bad news right from the get-go.
get shed of	get rid of	I need to get shed of that man; he's a pure drunk.
get straight	arrange matters	As soon as I get straight with Johnny, I'm gonna move out.
get up with	get in touch with	I couldn't get up with you on the phone, so I came over.

get your ducks in a row	organize things	I like to get my ducks in a row before I call a consultant.
give me a fit	cause pain	Doc, my back is giving me a fit.
give out	ended, ran out	My car just give out and died.
give out	tired	I'm just give out.
go away from here	die	I felt like I was going to go away from here.
go on	go away	Go on with your big talk.
go on	die	If my heart stops, let me just go on peaceful-like.
go to the bad	lose quality	O-rings will last for years before they go to the bad.
good piece	well-executed	That was a good piece of driving, getting through that last ice storm.
good to go	ready and waiting	Your car's good to go for that Missouri trip, Doc.
good to me	felt good	It seemed good to me when Billy accepted Jesus.
goozle	gizzard, esophagus	He got a piece of meat stuck in his goozle and like to have died.
got around	word spread	Don't let it get around that I've been here.

got away with	very upset	It got away with me when Momma went to jail.
got next to me	affected me deeply	It sure got next to me when Daddy died.
grand-young'uns	grandchildren	I got me three young-uns and six grand-young'uns.
groundpeas	peanuts	We got us some nice boiled groundpeas. Want some?
had went	had gone	I had went to the store but there weren't no one there.
hain't got the use of myself	powerless, feeble	He hain't got the use of hisself since he had that'ere stroke.
hairline	pubis (just below the bellybutton)	I got a rash from my chest clear down to my hairline.
handy as a shirt pocket	very useful	You brought your scouting knife? Man, you're handy as a shirt pocket.
hard-headed	stubborn, individualistic	She's hard-headed about going to the doctor.
hardly squeal	barely move or talk	He was hurt so bad he could hardly squeal.
hassling like a dog	short of breath	I was hassling like a dog out in your parking lot, Doc. Glad you let me in!
have a spasm	be upset	Norbert'll have a spasm when he hears I wrecked his car.

head	number of	He had eleven head of kids.
head knocker-over	emotional blow	The news of him a-dying was a real head knocker-over.
head rattle	nod head	Answer me out loud. I can't hear your head rattle.
heebie-jeebies	willies; total body budgies	I got the heebie jeebies jes' lookin' at him.
hell on hinges	outrageous	She was nothing but hell on hinges.
hen flew in ways	influenza	Ma's got that 'ere hen flew inways.
high blood	high blood pressure	The doctor said I had high blood.
high step	abnormal gait due to slap foot	I've been high stepping lately. Think my leg is paralyzed?
hissy fit	apoplectic seizure (very angry)	Mom'll have a hissy fit if she sees me with you.
hit	it	Hit weren't doing right, so I just chunked it.
hit me good	struck me forcefully	That medicine hit me good, and it holp me too.
hoed that row	been there, done that	Cancer? Doesn't frighten me. I've hoed that row twice already.

hog killing weather	very cold weather in the dead of winter	Any colder, and it'll be hog killing weather.
hold it in the road	be careful	You hold it in the road and come back safe, now!
holp	helped	That'ere medicine really holp me, Doc!
hoot and a holler	excitement	I've cut down smoking, but it's not worth a hoot and a holler.
hotter than the hinges of hell	very hot	It's hotter than the hinges of hell in here. Cain't you open the window a crack?
hot-natured	tends to feel warm	He's so hot-natured, he'll walk barefoot in the snow.
hush yo' mouf	be quiet	Hush yo' mouf, chile, the sheriff's coming!
huzzie	hussy	You painted huzzie, get away from my man!
hypertension	extreme anxiety	Give her some Valium Doc. She's got the hypertension bad.
I ain't lying	I'm lying (about to exaggerate)	I ain't lying, he's bigger'n a house.
I appreciate	I feel very good about	I appreciate all you've done, Doc.
I be so good	I feel fine	I be so good, I can't stand myself.

I declare	expletive (exclamation)	Suzie had her baby? Well, I declare!
I don't appreciate	I feel badly about	I don't appreciate your making that mistake and not admitting it.
I don't have a dog in that fight	It's not my concern	They're fussing over their salary, but I don't have a dog in that fight.
I'd know your hide in a tanning yard	You're familiar	You can't run from me. I'd know your hide in a tanning yard.
I thought she was clean	I thought she bathed occasionally and didn't have STD's	I only sleep with clean girls, Doc!
I'll be dawg'd	I'll be damned	Well, I'll be dawg'd. She really did come back!
I'll be doused	I'll be doggoned	I'll be doused if he ever goes back to her.
ill as a moccasin	nasty and vicious	She's been ill as a moccasin ever since her divorce.

ill as a wasp	highly irritable	She gets ill as a wasp this time of the month.
ill as a red-tailed wast (wasp)	even more irritable	see other "ill as"
ill-deformed	congenitally abnormal; mentally retarded	He was ill-deformed from the time he was born.
iller	more irritable	She's iller than a hornet without her Valium.
in a fix	in trouble	That tax-collector had me in a fix till I got me a lawyer.

in high cotton	doing well	We were in high cotton when the government gave us that van.
in moveable health	doing okay	I was in moveable health till this here stroke jumped on me.
in the run of the day	during a 24-hour period	I smoke a pack in the run of a day.
Is that a fact?	expletive	"Maude just died of cancer." "Is that a fact?"
It tickled me	I found it funny	It tickled me so good when Henrietta fell into the mud puddle.
jack your jaws	strike you hard	I'll jack your jaws if you talk to my wife again!
Jesus couldn't live with me	very irritable	I was so ill Jesus Christ couldn't live with me!
jittery as a paint shaker	nervous	That medicine made me as jittery as a paint shaker.
Joggin' in the Jug	fruit juice and vinegar mixture	Maude cleared out her veins with Joggin' in the Jug.
Johs'n County	Johnston County	Ah live in Johs'n County, Nor' Carolina.
Judgment Day on Monday	Like there was no tomorrow	Last Sunday Bob was swillin' liquor like it was Judgment Day on Monday.
jump a four-rail fence	energetic	I feel fine, Doc, like I could jump a four-rail fence.

jumped on me	developed an illness	This here artheritis jest jumped on me this morning.
jumped timing	lost control	I 'bout jumped timing when he told me that he slept with my wife.
just a couple of beers	two six-packs	I just had a couple of beers Doc, I ain't drunk.
keep	maintain	I keep a headache nowadays, since my sister moved in.
kick a wheel	I feel good	How you feeling, Charles? Like I could kick a wheel!
kick back	take it easy	When I retire, I'll just kick back and do nothing.
kick cover	have sex	Bobby and Sue been kickin' cover all week long.
kicking up sand	raising a fuss	What's he kickin' up sand about now?
kidneys acted	urinated	My kidneys acted good after that 'ere Lasix.

killed my britches	did me in	It near 'bout killed my britches when that car fell on me.
killing kind	lethal	What type of cancer did he have? The killing kind.
kindly	rather, kind of	She's kindly good natured, but watch her with the animals.
knocked me a-whining	struck me hard	When I complained, Pa knocked me a-whining.
lazy blood	indolence	I've got the tired blood, or the lazy blood, one.
leaders	tendons; ligaments	The leaders behind my knees is drawing up.
lick	blow	I took a lick in the head, Doc, and now I'm dizzy.
lick and a promise	short shrift/very brief	10 minutes a patient? Treating 'em with just a lick and a promise, aren't you!

You look
like someone
licked The red
off your candy

licked the red	sorely disappointed	What's the matter? You look like someone licked the red off your candy!
like	as in	He acted real friendly-like.
like 80 going north	a lot	That mammogram hurt like 80 going north.
like to	nearly	I like to have died when she came in with my husband.
little	skinny	My doctor's real little, but he's good.
live at	dwell	Susie, where do you live at? Need a ride?
long breath	deep breath	It hurts whenever I draw a long breath.
long on drywall, short on studs	not well put together mentally	Better count your change! That cashier's kindly long on drywall and short on studs.
long-tailed cat	very busy; hyper-alert	She's as busy as a long-tailed cat in a room full of rocking chairs.
look up to see the ground	feel depressed	I was so low I had to look up to see the ground.
Lord a massy	Lord have mercy	Lord a massy, honey, you looks marvelous.
love to	like to	I don't love to go to the doctor.
mad as fire	very angry	I was mad as fire when I found out he overcharged me.

mad itch	itchy rash	I've had the mad itch since taking that medicine.
make right	correct	I'll make it right by you, don't worry yourself none.
mash	press	Mash hard on the gas pedal honey, we're outta here!
mauling the rail	working hard and fast	The Hospital's got you mauling the rail, doc!
meanness	spitefulness (usually spoken in jest)	What causes that illness? Meanness, I guess.
mess	a concoction of unusual personality traits	Doc, you're a mess!
mess	collection	Ma cooked up a mess of collards.
might could	might be able to	I might could help you if I get some money.
Momonyms	Mother and the others	Momonyms at church, but they'll be by directly.

more times than a little	pretty often	I've heard people say "pyurt" more times than a little.
more times than a little	pretty often	I've heard people praise him more times than a little.
mule boiled in kerosene	untasty food	I'm so hungry I could eat a mule boiled in kerosene.
mule in the summertime	hard worker	The nurses on 2 East got rode like a mule in the summertime.
muley-headed	stubborn	You're a muley-headed old fool, that's what you are.
mulish	stubborn	He's mulish and won't listen to nobody.
murgans	many	Have some more peas! We've got murgans of them in the garden.
must have been a lie	senior moment	Forgot what I was going to say. Must have been a lie.
my goodness alive	expletive	My goodness alive child, you're as hungry as 3 newborn pigs!

names you don't hear up North	feminine	Robena, Lalon, Shakira, Matrid, Tanisha, Velia, Myrtie, Junnie Mae
	masculine	Durwood, Onnie, Roland, Jasper, Wilbert, Jim-Bob, Junior
nary	not	Have you got any maps? Nary a one.
nasty	disgusting	He brought in a pot full of all manner of nasty stuff.
near 'bout	nearly	He was near 'bout half grown.
nekkid	improperly naked	She was nekkid, pure nekkid!
nervous as a chicken	nervous and agitated	She was nervous as a chicken.
new rope	easily dissatisfied; very picky	You'd complain if you were hung with a new rope.
no 'count	lazy	You're a no good, no 'count shif'less SOB.

no pot to pee in	poor	He don't have a pot to pee in nor a window to throw it out of.
no raising	no proper rearing	Hush up. You ain't got no raising!
no way, shape form or fashion	no way	No way, shape, form or fashion are you going home till Doc says so.
nohow	anyhow	He didn't want it nohow.
not long	about two weeks	"How long have you had this chest pain?" "Not long."
not mighty good	terrible	I'm not feeling mighty good.
not worth killing	worthless	I'm old and wore out. Not worth killing, I guess.
nothin' extra	fair	How you feeling? Nothin' extra.

nutcracker	psychiatrist	Reckon I'll just have to see the nutcracker.
of a morning (night, etc.)	in the morning	I eat breakfast of a morning.
one	either or	He's downright mean, or stupid, one.
one-legged man	handicapped	He's about as useful as a one-legged man in a butt-kickin' contest.
onliest	only	He's the onliest banjo-picker I ever seen with two fingers.
passel	collection	I fixed me a passel of grits and sausage and took it to mama's house.
pat was in the Army	not long	He'll work on that about as long as Pat was in the army.
pea turkey	unidentifiable substance	Whatever he vomited up, you couldn't tell pea turkey from it.
pet dog	object of little value	I wouldn't send my pet dog to her, and he's made of concrete.
piddling	puttering around	Since I retired, I just piddle in the garden and around the house.
piddley	small, inconsequential	Don't bring that piddley mess here. Bring me some real food!

pig-pickin'	outdoor barbecue and pig roast	Congressman Daughtry's havin' a pig-pickin' tonight.
pin stroke	transient ischemic attack (TIA)	Pa's been having these pin strokes, but now it's the big 'n'.
pining over	grieving	Romeo was a-pining over Juliet when he kilt hisself.
pink rabbit	elusive item	I was so irritated I could catch a pink rabbit.
pip ginny	pimple	Her face is eat up with pip ginnies.
pitched over	fell over, leaned	He pitched slam over and blam! He hit the ground.
pitching woo	caressing each other	John 'n' Mary been pitching woo out on the porch swing.
place	farm	I live at ol' man Ranson's place.
playing outside the doghouse	sleeping around	George got caught playing outside the doghouse and now he's in for it!
plumb	purely	I'm plumb sick, is all.
poison	poison ivy	I got me a case of poison, Doc. Can you give me a shot for it?
pone	a skin nodule or lump	I got me a big ol' pone under my armpit.

powerful mess	a lot	He's in a powerful mess of trouble.
prayed to die	felt real bad	I prayed to die, but I lived instead.
pulling eye teeth	exceedingly difficult or painful	Getting my kids to clean house is like pulling eye teeth.
pure	veritable	She had a pure hissy-fit when the dog ate her pie.
put miles on	work hard, go far	I put a lot of miles on myself in a day's time.
put up	put away	Hain't you put up those samples yet?
puttin' in backer	tying and curing tobacco	Elsie was puttin' in backer when the alarm sounded.
pyuert	well, energetic	I feel right pyuert today.

raisin' sand	fussing	Stop raisin' sand. You'll get your turn!
rare back	lean back	He just rar'd back and went to sleep.
rattle when I walk	overmedicated	Doc, you've got me on so many pills, I pure rattle when I walk.
rawhide	very tough	She was tougher than new rawhide.
reckon	figure	I don't reckon I'll make it till tomorrow.
ridge runner	moonshiner escaping from revenooers	Jimmy F. was one famous ridge runner.
right	quite	I was right ready to fight, but Ma said no.
right good	extensive	I haven't seen him in a right good while.
right on	continuously	I've had this cold right on, and it gives me a fit.
right smart	a lot	Bobby licked him right smart, and now he's one sorry boo-boo.
risin'	boil	I've got risin's all over my body. Got some antibiotics for it? Or should I just use that ol' Black Salve?

Jimmy F was one
Famous Ridge Runner

rockin' chair rockin'	wasting energy	You're setting in a rockin' chair rockin', but you ain't goin' nowhere.
roto-tiller, beating like	vibrating fast	My heart went to beating like a roto-tiller, and then I fell out.
ruint	made weak, ruined	That medicine you gave me like to ruint me.
screwed and never kissed (a feminine xpression)	abused	I get screwed so much and never get kissed; it's pitiful!
see daylight	live	I still love to see daylight, even though I'm sickly.
see dirt thrown over	live longer than	Ma'll never die. She'll see dirt thrown over us.
seems good	felt good	It seemed good to me when that burn healed up.
set fields afire	spicy	Try this new ketchup. It'll set your fields on fire.
set my mouth right	concentrate properly	Couldn't open that apple jar. Guess I didn't set my mouth right.
settin' on a cactus	unpleasant	That MRI was more fun than settin' on a cactus.
seven year itch	slow	He bags them groceries slow as a seven year itch.
shake the sheets	look hard	You're so little, does your husband shake the sheets to find you?

...MORE fun Than settin' on a cactus

showed his butt	acted out impolitely	My son showed his butt at the movies when they told him to leave.
showed hisself	same as above	
showed his tail	same as above	(People show themselves a lot around here)
shug (shoog)	sweetie-pie	C'mere shug, and give your Aunt Lena a hug.
sick as a buzzard	very nauseated	I was sick as a buzzard, all day.
skeeters	mosquitoes	Them skeeters is eating me alive.
skin turned white	livid	He was so jealous his skin turned white.
slam	completely	I'm give slam out.
slap my jowls	expression of surprise	Well slap my jowls! Look what the wind blew in!
slinging a nasty	speed on a curve	Don't you sling a nasty, now. This road's slick!
slingin' out both drawer legs	dispensing rapidly	They were handing out Coke samples as fast as they could – slinging out both drawer legs!
slop jar	night basin, urinal	I feel like Death warmed over and left in a slop jar.
slop the hogs	feed the pigs	Mom's gone out to slop the hogs.

smoke a turkey	over 100 degrees Fahrenheit	They keep their house hot enough to smoke a turkey in.
smooth as Ex-Lax	real easy-like	The trip to Missouri went smooth as Ex-Lax.
snake'd bit me	right under my nose	There's my pencil! If it was a snake, it'd have bit me!
snap beans	string beans	Have some snap beans, honey.
snap beaned	emotionally overwrought	Mama's all snap beaned over Dawg's death.
snot	innards	I'll beat (or worry) the snot out of him.
some'eres	somewhere	Some'eres in here I got my pocket knife.
somethin' bad	intensely	He wanted that girl somethin' bad.
somethin' in the world	special	Well, ain't that somethin' in the world!
sooner mutt	nondescript	Pedigree? Nah. He's a sooner mutt. He'd sooner be one as another.
sore pain	tender to the touch	It's not an ache, Doc, just a sore pain.
sore-tail cats	very irritable	Him and her get along like two sore-tail cats.
sorry	low quality, lazy	You're a sorry excuse for a man.

sorry as owlpoop	low quality	Bet you think I'm sorrier'n owlpoop, but I can't go no faster.
sow and seven pigs	a lot of food	After dinner, my belly looked like I ate a sow and seven pigs.
spit cup	spittoon (Dixie cup with tissue inside)	Fetch me my spit cup, shug, this here backer's got me foamin' at the mouth.
spit fire	hot mouth	After those chili peppers, I felt like I'd spit fire.
stay	live	Where do you stay?
stick a fork in	finished	You can stick a fork in me, 'cause I'm done!
stirring about	moving about	My joints hurt of a morning till I get to stirring about.
stomach upset	diarrhea	That virus upset his stomach somethin' fierce.
stomp-down drunk	very drunk	He was stomp-down drunk.

stove up	unintentionally made pregnant	Julie got stove up by Jonathan, and now he's done gone!
straight up and down	exact copy	That painting is just like the old tobacco barn, straight up and down.
striking paper	toilet paper	Fetch me some striking paper, honey. We're out.
study on it	analyze carefully	Doc. W. wants me to have a heart cath. I'm studying on it.

Give me some sugar

sugar	a kiss	C'mere little Annie, and gimme some sugar.
sugar	diabetes	Doc says I got to watch what I eat 'cause I got sugar.
sunday-go-to-meetin'	dressed up	She was all Sunday-go-to-meetin' when she answered the door.
sure do, sure do	affirmative	Do we sell strawberries? Sure do, sure do.
sure don't	really don't	Do we sell maps? Sure don't. Try next door.
swanee	swear	I swanee, I'll never lend him money again.
sweeper	vacuum cleaner	Fetch the sweeper and clean the rug, honey. My ash tray fell to the floor.
swimmy-headed	dizzy	After taking that-'ere medicine, I got right swimmy-headed.
tail hole	anus	I have to wipe his tail-hole day and night.
take spells of	occasionally	My leg'll take spells of itching.

"MA WAS WRAPPED TIGHT
AS A BANJO STRING."

take this to the bank	count on it	You can take this to the bank, there's nothing better.
tales out of school	inappropriate talk	I ain't tellin' no tales out of school, Doc, but she's selling that Vicodin you gave her!
tar	pep	That flu just took the tar out of me.
'taters	potatoes	Fetch me them arsh 'taters, Sue Ellen.
tell you what's true	this is a fact	I'll tell you what's true, he's no doctor at all.
tender-hearted	compassionate, sensitive	She's real tender-hearted, so be easy on her.
that's a dead soldier	that's no longer useful	She put away the empty medicine vial, saying "That's a dead soldier."
that-'ere	that-there	Bring me that-'ere medicine bottle, honey.
there's not but	there's only	There's not but one doctor in this town.
tight as a banjo string	very nervous, tense	Ma was wrapped tight as a banjo string before the wedding.
tight as a tick	very swollen	My leg was swole up tighter'n a tick.
to be sure	no way	To be sure, you're not going to charge me $25 for this visit!

too good	too well	I didn't like it too good, neither.
took a-hurting	began to hurt	My leg took a-hurtin' real bad.
took hold	seized	He took hold of that bar and twisted it good.
tore up	disordered	That cabbage sure tore my stomach up.
tore all to pieces	in disarray	It tore me all to pieces when my uncle died.
toucheous	painful to the touch	Ow! That spot there's mighty toucheous!
travelling fart	lot of GI gas pains	She had her a travelling fart, but that Mylanta holp her.
trick	machine, gadget	I bought me a trick to measure my blood pressure with.
ugly	impolite	She was real ugly to me on the phone, so I hung up on her.
up and	suddenly, determinedly	So they up and they took and they moved to Beverly. Hills, that is.
used to be	landmark	Make a left just past where K-mart used to be.

want in one hand, crap in the other	you can't have it	You want ice cream before dinner? You've got want in one hand, and crap in the other. See which one fills up first.
warmed over Death	bad	I feel like warmed over Death left two weeks in a slop jar.
water-tight tail hole	of course	Can I fix cars? Does a fish have a water-tight tail hole?
weak as a puppy	very weak	I been weak as a puppy ever since the flu took hold of me.
weren't	wasn't	Hit weren't doin' right, so I chunked it.
which it	which	I own a '66 Volvo, which it ain't pretty, but it runs good.
wild hair	stray hair	I got a wild hair in my eye.
windowshade	rapidly moving	My sugar went up and down like a windowshade.
work a dozen	labor intensive	One sick man will work a dozen to death.
workingest	most active	You the workingest man I ever seen.

worry	bother	He worried the pure shrinking life out of me.
worth five cent	worthless, spoiled rotten	That child ain't worth five cent.
wrappin' the road	travelling a lot	I been wrapping the road between Garner and Kenly on my way to work.
wrong as two left shoes	very improper	You treated a drug rash with penicillin? That's as wrong as two left shoes.
yeah boy	affirmative, emphatic encouragement	"I fed the mules today, Pop." "Yeah, boy!"
yonder	there	Yonder's my boy, on top of that tractor.
you can't deny him	your child looks like you	Is that your boy? You can't deny him!
young'uns	children	Bring the young'uns to church, all right? They'll have a good time.

V.C. (call him Cullum) Rogers did the illustrations, including this self-portrait!